H22.869.352.3

KOOIJMAN, S
HJ   9/88

Polynesian
barkcloth
2.50

HERTFORDSHIRE LIBRARY SERVICE
Please return this book on or before the
last date shown or ask for it to be renewed

L.32/rev.'81   I

CENTRAL RESOURCES
LIBRARY
01707-281530

10/12

D1344292

SHIRE ETHNOGRAPHY

2

Cover photograph
Strips of paper mulberry bark are beaten out by a team of women under the leadership of Silipa, the chief's wife (in front). The photograph was taken in the village of Nasau on Mothe Island, Fiji, on 19th June 1973. It shows the initial phase of the beating process. The situation is rather exceptional since each woman usually works by herself on her own anvil or *ndundua*. Here, the women give a demonstration of *veilali*, rhythmic beating. (See also figure 30.)

British Library Cataloguing in Publication Data available

To the people of Mothe Island, Fiji, without whose cooperation and friendship this book could not have been written.

HERTFORDSHIRE
LIBRARY SERVICE

746.0454

Published by
SHIRE PUBLICATIONS LTD
Cromwell House, Church Street, Princes Risborough
Aylesbury, Bucks HP17 9AJ, UK

Series Editor: Bryan Cranstone

Copyright © Simon Kooijman, 1988
All rights reserved.
No part of this publication may be reproduced or transmitted in any form or by any means, electronic or mechanical, including photocopy, recording, or any information storage and retrieval system, without permission in writing from the publishers.

ISBN 0 85263 943 0

First published 1988

Set in 11 point Times and printed in Great Britain by
C. I. Thomas & Sons (Haverfordwest) Ltd,
Press Buildings, Merlins Bridge, Haverfordwest, Dyfed.

Contents

Acknowledgements

This book is based on research in museum collections and on fieldwork in Polynesia and Fiji which were made possible by the financial support of the Nederlandse Organisatie voor Zuiverwetenschappelijk Onderzoek (Netherlands Organisation for the Advancement of Pure Research), the Nederlandse Stichting voor Wetenschappelÿk Onderzoek van de Tropen (Netherlands Foundation for the Advancement of Tropical Research), and the Wenner Gren Foundation for Anthropological Research in New York.

Permission to publish photographs of tapas in their collections was kindly granted by: the Auckland War Memorial Museum, Auckland, New Zealand; the Bernice Pauahi Bishop Museum, Honolulu, Hawaii; the Museum of Mankind, London; the Peabody Museum, Salem, Massachusetts; and the Rijksmuseum voor Volkenkunde (National of Museum of Ethnology), Leiden, Netherlands.

My thanks are due to Mr I. C. Brussee of the Rijksmuseum voor Volkenkunde for the processing and the reproduction of the photographic material. When not otherwise stated, the photographs were taken by the author during his museum research and fieldwork.

4

List of illustrations

1
Introduction

Geography of Polynesia

Polynesia, the 'many islands', is part of a region which has been called Oceania since the beginning of the nineteenth century. The ocean was named *mar del sur* by Balboa, the Spanish explorer who, crossing the Isthmus of Darien in Panama in 1513, saw the sea before him stretching in a southerly direction. Magellan, the first European to sail across this vast expanse of water in 1520-1, gave it the name *mare pacifico:* Pacific Ocean is the term commonly used today.

The Polynesian islands (figure 1) form an equilateral triangle, sometimes called the 'Polynesian triangle', with angles at Hawaii in the north, Easter Island in the east and New Zealand in the south. The length of each side equals the distance from London to Bombay. However, the total land area of the islands scattered over this part of the Pacific (excluding New Zealand and including Fiji) is only 63,647 sq km (24,577 square miles) which is about 75 per cent of the land area of Scotland. Fiji is included as a transitional area between Polynesia and Melanesia because of its cultural ties with Tonga, in particular regarding the making and decoration of barkcloth and its role in society.

In the western Pacific the boundary between the continent and the ocean does not coincide structurally with the coast but lies hundreds of miles out to sea. Here a wide series of island arcs has been formed, stretching from the Aleutians to New Zealand. Japan, the Philippines, New Guinea and New Zealand are examples of extensive, mountainous islands and archipelagoes. The Fiji archipelago, lying on two partly submerged platforms, also belongs to this group of 'continental' islands. On many islands in this western margin of the Pacific the mountains are of volcanic origin: a number of the island arcs alternate with deep submarine trenches.

The Polynesian islands east of Fiji are not structurally connected with the Asian continent. They are spread over the expanse of ocean 'like a handful of confetti scattered over a lake'. Two groups can be distinguished, the 'high islands' and the 'low islands'. The former, the Hawaii Islands, the archipelagoes of Samoa and Tahiti (Society Islands) and some of the southern Cook Group, consist of volcanic piles standing high out of the water, forming mountains. The trade winds controlling the climate between latitudes 30 degrees north and south rise along the slopes of these mountains and supply plenty of rain. This enables abundant tropical vegetation to grow on the fertile erosion soils of the volcanic rock. It is only here, on the high islands, that the condition of the soil and the amount of rainfall allow the cultivation of the paper mulberry, the main source of barkcloth. Polynesian culture reached its highest level of development on these islands with their favourable natural resources: good fertile soil for food production, stone for making tools and wood for canoe building.

The great majority of the Polynesian islands are low islands, however. They have a volcanic, basaltic core which in most cases is below sea-level. The visible part of such an island is a mass of limestone coral reefs, built up by marine lime-secreting animals, the most important of which is the coral polyp.

Natural resources

The characteristic Pacific coral island consists of a circular reef or atoll, many of which rise no more than 3-6 metres (10-20 feet) above sea-level. The reef is usually broken by a number of passages and so forms a ring of tiny islands surrounding a lagoon. The diameter of an atoll can range, approximately, from 1 to 200 km (0.6 to 125 miles). The possibilities for horticulture are very limited because the layer of erosion soil on the sandy limestone is thin and poor and rainfall is insufficient. Of the variety of Pacific root crops mentioned below, only one inferior taro species can be grown, while the only trees found on atolls are the coconut palm and the *Pandanus* and wood for building seaworthy outrigger canoes was in many cases not available. Neither was the basaltic island rock suitable for axes and other tools. It is these low islands which suffer most from the hurricanes which frequently occur in the western part of the Pacific.

Four species of root crops provide the basic food of Oceania: the taro (*Colocasia esculenta*), the yam (*Dioscorea alata*), the kumara or sweet potato and the manioc or cassava (*Manihot utilissima* [*M. esculenta*]). Taro and yam were introduced from the west in prehistoric times, as was probably the kumara (its alleged American provenance having been refuted by the results of botanical and linguistic research). Starchy food is also provided by the fruit of the breadfruit tree (*Artocarpus altilis* [*A. communis*]), available in abundance for many months of the year. Seafaring immigrants from the West brought the breadfruit and, probably, the *Pandanus* and the coconut palm.

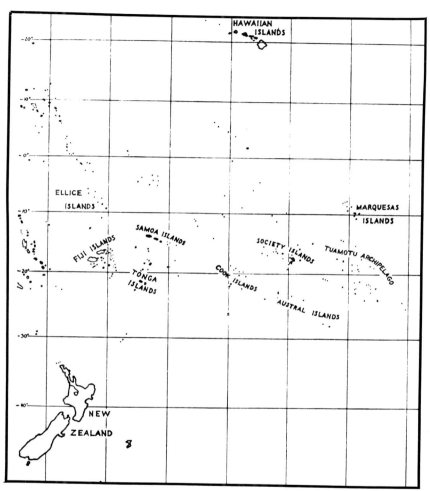

1. Sketch map of Polynesia, showing the main island groups.

The coconut palm is closely connected with human life on the islands. The fat-rich liquid from the flesh is indispensable for cooking fish and vegetables and the water is essential for drinking purposes, particularly on the low islands and on boat trips and fishing expeditions. The leaves are used for thatching roofs and for the manufacture of mats and baskets. The husk of a particular kind of coconut palm is suitable for the production of sennit cord, which is important as lashing material in the construction of houses and canoes. The flesh of old coconuts is dried and sold as copra, which for many island communities is the main source of cash income.

Another plant the ancestors of the Polynesians carried with them on their voyages was the paper mulberry (*Broussonetia papyrifera*), the source of barkcloth. It can grow only on the high islands.

The animals introduced by the seafarers were the pig, the dog and the jungle fowl. Fish is by far the most important protein-rich food. Fishing and horticulture are the two principal components of the traditional subsistence economy.

Linguistic and cultural origins

The Polynesian languages belong to the Austronesian or Malayo-Polynesian language family, which extends geographically from Madagascar to Easter Island and from Taiwan and Hawaii in the north to New Zealand. Its relationship with languages in the Far East, notably Thailand, has been demonstrated. This linguistic evidence is one of the strongest arguments against Thor Heyerdahl's theory of the American origin of the Polynesians and the Polynesian culture. (See Heyerdahl, *American Indians in the Pacific,* and relevant sections in the works of such specialists as Suggs and Bellwood.) No scholarly support is given to the idea of an American origin for the Polynesians.

Migrations

The long migratory voyage from the Asian mainland through the 'Indonesian Mediterranean' and out into the open ocean lasted many generations. This movement was by no means a continuous stream: it was frequently interrupted by the seafarers settling down for a generation or longer on islands they encountered on their way. Nevertheless, these eastward migrations, covering a distance of almost two-fifths of the circumference of the globe, from the coasts of Asia to Easter Island, form probably the greatest marine enterprise in the history of mankind. The Polynesians therefore fully deserve the title 'Vikings of the sunrise' bestowed on them by Peter H. Buck, a pioneer in the study of the traditional cultures of Oceania, though their achievements as seafarers and colonists surpass by far those of their European predecessors.

The seafaring canoes of the Polynesian islands can be divided into two major classes: the single-outrigger and the double-hull canoes. The basic shape of both types was a hollowed-out tree

2. Tongan canoes. After a drawing made by William Hodges in October 1773 during Cook's second voyage.

trunk, with gunwale planks attached to the hull. Provided with a mast carrying the characteristic, triangular mat sail, a platform and a cabin, the craft were steered by one or two long paddles. These vessels often had an impressive size: James Cook mentions a Tahitian canoe which was somewhat longer than his own ship, the *Endeavour,* which had a length of 35 metres (115 feet).

The double-hull canoe played an important role in the settlement of the Polynesian islands. The first European sailor to sight this kind of vessel was Willem Schouten. In his journal he describes and illustrates a double-hull canoe, that is, a *tongiaki,* sighted when his ship, the Dutch *Zeehaen,* passed north of the Tonga Islands on her way across the Pacific from the Magellan Straits to the Moluccas in 1616. Abel Tasman also saw a *tongiaki* in 1643, devoting two pages of his journal to a description with illustrations. A fine accurate drawing of such a canoe was made by William Hodges, draughtsman and artist during Cook's second expedition (1772-5) (figure 2). The Polynesians ceased to make these proud vessels in the late nineteenth century, though the type survived for longer in Fiji, where a few double-hull canoes were built in the first half of the twentieth century. Some of these Fijian canoes had remarkable dimensions: the largest could carry more than two hundred people. The steering paddle of such a canoe was often more than 10 metres (30 feet) long and had to be handled by several crew members simultaneously. It could sail before the wind at a speed of 20 km (12 miles) an hour.

The large travelling canoes in Polynesia and Fiji bore as provisions tubers, *Pandanus* fruits, coconuts, live birds for meat and drinking water stored in large bamboos and gourds, sufficient for a voyage of three to four weeks, enough time to cover the longest distance between islands. Also carried were seedlings of plants, trees and tubers, as well as pigs, dogs and jungle fowl.

The Polynesian sailors were skilled navigators over wide spaces of open sea. Stars were their guides at night and during the day they used as pilots land birds, such as the noddy and the frigate bird, which fly out to their fishing grounds in the morning, over distances of 30-80 km (20-50 miles), and return to an island in the evening. Thus islands could be traced which were far beyond the horizon. An as yet invisible island was also located by the cloud forming above its surface in the heat of the day, while in addition slight changes in the ocean swell revealed the existence of an unsighted island. The Polynesian canoes could sail close to the wind and were able to change tack so that they could head into the wind. In periods of calm they were paddled.

What motivations explain the spread of population over the hundreds of islands in the enormous Polynesian triangle? One of the main reasons will have been overpopulation: even on the fertile high islands the available resources would have set a limit to population increase. War was certainly another motive: the vanquished party were sometimes given the opportunity to save themselves by setting sail for another island. The custom of primogeniture (the chief being succeeded by his eldest son) also led to migration. At the death of their father, the younger sons were deprived of any form of chiefly power and often attempted to lead a group of adventurous men and their families with them to another island.

The discovery of hitherto unknown islands was accidental. Whether the Polynesian seafarers were able to undertake purposeful voyages once an island or a group of islands were settled has been a subject of research by students of Oceanic migrations. Andrew Sharp has attempted to demonstrate that such voyages were made only within a distance of 500 km (300 miles) and were therefore restricted to four island clusters (the Tonga-Samoa-Fiji group, the Society and Tuamotu islands, the Hawaii archipelago and the Marquesas). These ideas may be criticised, however, in the light of more recent work. The experiences of David Lewis on board a Micronesian outrigger canoe in the late 1960s, for example, open new perspectives on sailing and navigation in the Pacific. He accompanied a native

3. A human sacrifice on Tahiti. Engraving by W. Woollett after a drawing by John Webber (Johann Weber) made in September 1777 during Cook's third voyage.

crew making a return voyage of more than 650 km (400 miles) between two island clusters in Micronesia. The details of the admirable skill of these sailors, as presented in Lewis's book, provide firm ground for the hypothesis that the ancient seafarers of Oceania, Micronesia and Polynesia were also able to cover the long distances of open ocean between the island clusters.

The influx of settlers into Polynesia, coming from their ancient homeland in Asia, penetrated Indonesia. The occurrence in

4. War fleet assembled at Pare, east of Pape'ete, Tahiti. Painting made by William Hodges in May 1774 during Cook's second voyage.

5. Death of Captain James Cook at Kealakekua Bay, Hawaii, on 14th February 1779. After a drawing by John Webber.

Melanesia of prehistoric artefacts (such as pottery, stone adzes and shell knives) related to those of the early culture of the western Polynesians is one of the indications that the Melanesian islands were settled next. The Tonga group were the first islands in Polynesia to be occupied by the immigrants, which took place after 1500 BC. Over the following two thousand years their descendants spread over the remainder of the Polynesian triangle.

Tonga-Samoa was the first population dispersal centre. Later Tahiti (Society Islands) and the Marquesas played a similar role in populating the peripheral islands in the north, east and south. New Zealand was settled around AD 1000 by migrants probably originating from Tahiti. It is likely that Easter Island was occupied from the Marquesas in the fourth century AD.

European exploration

In the light of these achievements the claim of Westerners to have 'discovered' the Pacific islands is misleading. During the peak period of exploration and colonisation in Oceania, European sailors did not venture beyond the landlocked Mediterranean and the coasts of the Atlantic, the Vikings' adventures in the north of that ocean coinciding with the final thrust of the

Polynesians from the already settled islands in the centre of the triangle into New Zealand on the periphery.

The 'European discoveries' are, however, relevant in that the coming of the white explorers marked the beginning of a time of Westernisation and change which was also a period of observation of traditional cultures, including the manufacture, decoration and uses of barkcloth. The era of European discoveries may be subdivided into periods of domination: the sixteenth century (the Spanish), the seventeenth century (the Dutch) and the eighteenth century (the English and the French). It ended with the three expeditions of Captain James Cook in the years 1768-79 (figures 3-5). After these the topography of the vast island-strewn ocean was known in all its main features. Although for the Western powers involved the material gain may have been disappointing, the knowledge of the people, the animal life and the flora of Oceania gathered by the scientists participating in Cook's expeditions form a still unexhausted source of information. (Further details of the Europeans in the Pacific may be found in the works of J. L. Beaglehole and Douglas L. Oliver.)

6. Paper mulberry garden on Mothe Island, Fiji.

2
Tapa in Polynesia

Tapa making is now a lost art in many parts of Polynesia. Where it is still made and decorated, and plays a part in society, tapa is associated with the traditional aspects of life. Though the techniques of manufacture and decoration, as well as its function, have experienced foreign influences, tapa has essentially remained a traditional phenomenon.

Barkcloth from Oceania, as well as from other tropical regions, is designated 'tapa'. The use of this term for barkcloth was originally restricted to a few areas: Mangareva and Hawaii. On the Hawaiian Islands the word *kapa* (the Hawaiian version of the general Polynesian form) was part of the traditional vocabulary; it also meant edge, border or boundary. Similar meanings for 'tapa' are given in many other Polynesian languages. On Samoa, for instance, the uncoloured border of a coloured sheet of barkcloth is called *tapa*, the name for the cloth being *siapo;* this term is also used on the surrounding islands (Uvea, Niue and the Hoorn Islands). *Hiapo* was the word for barkcloth on the Marquesas Islands, while the Tahitians used the designation *ahu* and the Tongans *ngatu*. The Fijian word is *masi*, whereas the Tongan *ngatu* is in use, for special categories of cloth, in the eastern Lau Group where Tongan influence is felt.

The term 'tapa' was introduced as a general denotation for any Polynesian barkcloth, regardless of its provenance, in the early nineteenth century, when British, French and American whalers had appeared in Polynesia and made their bases and supply stations in Hawaii, Tahiti, the Marquesas, Samoa and New Zealand. Among the curios acquired and taken home by the whaling crews were pieces of barkcloth, called *kapa* in Hawaii and *tapa* in Samoa. These mariners, both European and American sailors and native crew members (especially Hawaiians), were responsible for the spread of the term 'tapa', which became generally accepted. Under this name barkcloth from Polynesia found its way to museums and private collections in Europe and the United States, where the term was universally accepted for the designation of barkcloth, including material from other tropical regions: Indonesia, Africa and South America.

The trees providing the material for barkcloth in Polynesia belong to the family Moraceae and, specifically, to the genera

Broussonetia, Artocarpus and *Ficus.* Of these the *Broussonetia papyrifera* or paper mulberry (figure 6) is most commonly used for the highest quality cloth. The plant is indigenous to eastern Asia, from where it was probably spread as a source of barkcloth, together with barkcloth manufacture, to Indochina, Thailand and Burma. From there it was carried by emigrants to Indonesia, where tapa techniques reached a high degree of development on Java and among the Toraja of the central part of Celebes (Sulawesi). The voyagers setting out from Indonesia, whose descendants were to settle on the Polynesian islands, took paper mulberry cuttings with them in their canoes, carefully preserved in damp earth or bark. The plant was unable to maintain itself in the poor natural environment of the atolls and could flourish only on the high volcanic islands with their fertile soil and abundant, regular rainfall. The paper mulberrry tree was cultivated for the purpose of tapa manufacture and still is in those areas of Polynesia where tapa production has survived.

The *Artocarpus* (breadfruit tree) was also introduced into Polynesia in prehistoric times. It is primarily a source of food, though its bark is used for the production of tapa of lower quality. *Ficus* trees grow wild and are probably native to the Pacific; as a source of barkcloth they are now of little importance.

Though restricted to the high islands where the paper mulberry could be cultivated, tapa making spread all over Polynesia. The techniques of manufacture and decoration share a number of common elements, or a general basic pattern. Nevertheless, regional differences existed, particularly between the islands in the centre and north, and western Polynesia. These differences will be discussed in a presentation of tapa and its role in island societies characteristic of both areas: Tahiti (Society Islands) and Hawaii in central and northern Polynesia, and Mothe Island in the Lau Group of Fiji, in the west. The choice of a Fijian island as an example typical of western Polynesia is justified by the Tongan cultural influences that are manifest in the Lau Islands, particularly regarding the manufacture of a special kind of barkcloth and its social and ceremonial functions. (Tapa on Mothe was the subject of the author's field research in 1973 and full information on this topic is therefore available.)

3
Tahiti

Manufacture of tapa

The main source of the bark used for making *ahu*, the native name for tapa, was the paper mulberry (*aute*) which was cultivated in special gardens. Other trees used for this purpose were the *Artocarpus* or breadfruit (*uru*) and two *Ficus* species. The *aute* bark gave a white tapa of very good quality which was primarily worn by persons of high rank. Tapa made from the *Artocarpus* and *Ficus* trees was not as white and soft as the *aute* tapa and was mainly worn by people of lower rank. A special kind of tapa made from *Ficus* bark was much valued, however. It was believed to have been a gift of the gods to mankind and was used to adorn the large figures of deities on the *marae*, especially that of Oro, the principal divinity of ancient Tahiti. The description of the manufacture of tapa given here refers to the processing of the *aute* bark. This was highly elaborate and time-consuming and thus easily attracted the attention of the late eighteenth-century and early nineteenth-century European observers to whom we owe our knowledge of Tahitian tapa.

After the paper mulberry tree had been cut, the bark as a whole (the outer bark together with the inner bark) was stripped from the trunk. It was then soaked for several days to make it softer and more flexible, after which the green outer bark was scraped from the inner bark. The damp inner bark was then wrapped in plantain leaves and left to ferment for three days. By carefully arranging the strips a coherent mass of fibres, about 10 metres (30 feet) long and 30 cm (1 foot) wide, was formed. This was then beaten by groups of two to three hundred women under the supervision of the wives of the chiefs. When these tapas were finished, they sometimes had a width of almost 4 metres (13 feet) and could be up to 200 metres (650 feet) long. This kind of tapa was made for ceremonial occasions, that is for presentation to chiefs and nobles, as described below.

When tapa was made for household use, the strips of inner bark were beaten separately. Larger sheets were obtained by the beater felting together the overlapping borders or top ends of the beaten strips.

Both the beaters (*ie*) and the anvils (*tutu, tutua*) used for this work were made of wood. The *tutu* were thick planks 6-9 metres (20-30 feet) long, made of wood selected for its hardness as well as for a pleasant and melodious sound produced by the beaters. The beaters were four-sided mallets with rounded handles about 35 cm (14 inches) long (figure 7). The four beating surfaces bore parallel longitudinal grooves with a constant spacing. The width and depth of the grooves varied from one surface to another, the average number of grooves on the four surfaces being 10-17-23-40. The beating was started with the *ie* surface bearing the coarsest grooving and the width of the material increased rapidly but also became indented with the coarse ridges. As the work continued and the *ahu* became thinner, the finer beating surfaces were used successively. The material was saturated with water for the entire beating process. When the work was interrupted it was wrapped in thick green leaves.

In addition to the long ceremonial *ahu* made by beating out the fermented, coherent fibre mass, and the much smaller household tapas produced by the beating and felting together of separate bark strips, Tahitian women made a thick but still pliant kind of *ahu* by felting and pasting together very carefully prepared pieces of barkcloth. The result of this procedure was a tapa feeling like thin chamois leather, the original paper-like layers of which could still be distinguished.

Decoration of tapa

For the decoration of their tapas the women had a number of natural dyes at their disposal. The range of colours included red, brown, yellow and black, with a large number of shades of, and between, red and brown. Red dyes consisted of a mixture of the juice prepared from one of the *Ficus* species used for the making of tapa and coconut water. (The women who made these dyes had red fingertips and nails, an effect which was sometimes

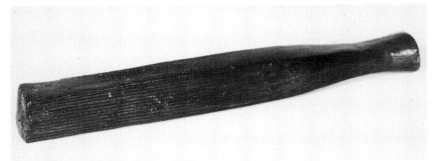

7. Tahitian tapa beater *(ie),* showing the surface with coarsest grooving. (Simon Kooijman; photograph: Rijksmuseum voor Volkenkunde, Leiden.)

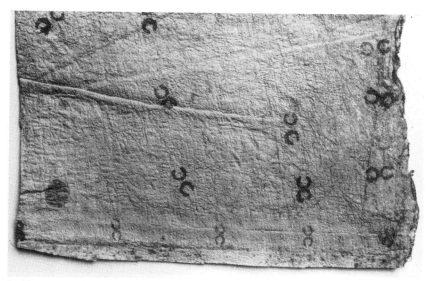

8. Fragment of Tahitian tapa; ecru and brown. Probably late eighteenth century. (Museum of Mankind, London.)

obtained deliberately.) A reddish brown dye was made from the bark of the *Casuarina* tree or the candlenut tree (*Aleurites moluccana*). Sources of yellow dyes included the root of the *nono* bush (*Morinda forsteri, M. citrifolia*), the fruit of the *tamanu* tree (*Calophyllum inophyllum*), a kind of pepper (*Piper methysticum*) from which the Polynesian beverage called *kava* was obtained, and the turmeric or *reya* (*Curcuma viridiflora*), which was also used here, as in many parts of Oceania, for painting the body. A black dye was made from the sap of a mountain plantain although, for colouring an entire sheet black, the tapa was buried in wet, swampy soil under the roots of a coconut palm for two or three days. Reddish brown dyes from the *Casuarina* and the candlenut tree, and yellow and red dyes, were also used to colour an entire piece of cloth. The tapas were first immersed in the dye and then spread in the sun to dry. The wearing of plain yellow and red tapas was the privilege of high-ranking people. Solid-colour tapas were also made by colouring one side of the cloth. A layer of red or yellow dye was applied to the tapa.

Many of these tapas were decorated. The decoration of the oldest known Tahitian tapas (those collected about 1780) consists of an irregular pattern of small, circular designs (figure 8). Semicircles and simple designs made by combinations of circles

9. Fern leaf pattern on a Tahitian tapa; ecru and brown. (Peabody Museum, Salem, Massachusetts.)

and semicircles, or both, also occur. According to the observations of J. R. Forster, the naturalist who accompanied James Cook on his second voyage and who was in Tahiti in 1773-4, these designs were applied to the tapa with the circular cut end of a piece of bamboo dipped in a dye.

A new style of tapa decoration, though based on a similar technique, developed in the last quarter of the eighteenth century. Tapas from that period are often decorated with delicate leaf motifs. Fern leaf motifs (figure 9) predominate but patterns consisting of a combination of fern prints and prints of other leaves also occur (figure 10). Fern frond prints were sometimes combined with a design of angular geometric figures. According to the missionary William Ellis, who was in Tahiti from 1817 until the early 1820s, 'the leaf, or flower, is laid carefully on the dye; as

10. Print of scale moss on a Tahitian tapa; ecru and brown. (Auckland Institute and Museum, Auckland.)

soon as the surface is covered with the colouring matter, the stained leaf or flower, with its leaflets or petals correctly adjusted, is fixed on the cloth, and pressed gradually and regularly down. When it is removed, the impression is beautiful and clean.'

It is impossible to be certain of the reasons for this new development in tapa decoration. It did, however, originate in the early contact period when Western influences made themselves felt. It is conceivable that the patterns on printed calicoes of Indian origin, which could have been brought to Tahiti by English seamen, may have contributed to this new style of decoration. In 1797 the missionary ship *Duff* brought the '*Duff* missionaries' of the London Missionary Society to Tahiti. This event marked the beginning of the era of Christianisation and Westernisation which brought with it, among other things, an increasing flow of Western commodities, particularly textiles. The import of woven cloth, together with the missionaries' negative attitude towards the religious and ceremonial aspects of tapa, led to the extinction of this traditional handicraft by the middle of the nineteenth century.

During this period of transition, which covered the first three or four decades of the nineteenth century, new relations were established between Tahiti and islands in western Polynesia, especially Samoa, after the expansion of the London Missionary Society from Tahiti to the Samoan Archipelago. This relationship is reflected in foreign, western Polynesian elements appearing in the decorative patterns of Tahitian tapas made in this period. On the other hand, tapa manufacture in Samoa was enriched by this contact with Tahiti since Samoan women started to make ponchos after the example of the Tahitian *tiputa*.

Uses of tapa

In ancient Tahiti tapa was important as a material for clothing. Most commonly worn by both men and women was the poncho or *tiputa*, a rectangular strip of tapa about 3 metres (10 feet) long and 90 cm (3 feet) wide, with a hole in the centre (*tiputa*, to pierce, pierced). The hole was the opening for the head, the garment hanging down over the front and the back of the wearer and reaching to about the knee.

In this hierarchical society, wide differences in quality of clothing existed, according to the social rank of the wearer. Chiefs and nobles wore ponchos consisting of several paper-thin layers of tapa felted and pasted together, with a very fine, bleached top layer. In early nineteenth-century Tahiti this type of tapa bore printed leaf designs. Also mentioned is an additional decoration of feathers and rosettes of red and black seeds. The *tiputa* worn by people of lower rank were generally made without any special care and left undecorated. Underneath the *tiputa,* as underclothing, the men wore a *maro,* a long strip of tapa that was wrapped around the waist and drawn between the legs. The women's underwear consisted of the *pau* or *pareu,* 'a piece of cloth about two yards long, which was drawn round the waist and fastened jauntily on one side, falling like a petticoat to the calf of the leg'. *Maro* and *pau* were generally undecorated. Women of rank might don a fine, decorated shawl or scarf-like garment which was thrown around the body and fastened over one shoulder. As previously, the wearing of red and yellow dyed tapas was the prerogative of the higher ranks.

Long strips of undecorated, brilliantly white tapa made by the communal efforts of two to three hundred women, and sometimes measuring as much as 180 metres (600 feet) in length, also served as a sign of wealth and a status symbol for the chiefly class. When such a tapa was ceremonially presented to a chief, it was wrapped around the body of a young man or woman, forming a white cylinder around the torso about 5 metres (16 feet) in circumference, which could only be carried with great difficulty. These extremely long, plain white tapas, rolled up and wrapped in matting, were a visible sign of the chief's prosperity and position during his life and accompanied his body after death.

These bundles, called *ruru vehe,* were not only in the possession of important persons but were also found in the buildings where sacred objects and the gods' images were kept. They were therefore also, and perhaps primarily, an attribute of the gods, especially of Oro, the principal god of Tahiti.

4
Hawaii

Manufacture of tapa

The physical environment on the Hawaiian islands provided such an abundant variety of plants that there was an inexhaustible supply of the material for making barkcloth. Here also, the paper mulberry (*wauke*) was the most important source from which the finest-quality tapa was made. The *wauke* was cultivated: the plant stood in the sugar-cane and banana plantations, but there were also sometimes special *wauke* gardens where the young plants were protected from the wind by sheltering enclosures and the soil was fertilised by rotting leaves. Young shoots of the *Artocarpus* (*uru*) were also used. The *Ficus*, which was an essential element in the tapa production of ancient Tahiti, is not mentioned in connection with the barkcloth of Hawaii.

The Hawaiian women had, however, at their disposal tapa-supplying plants, growing wild on the islands, which were not available in the rest of Polynesia. The most important of these was the *mamaki* (*Pipturus* sp.), a shrub or, in rare cases, a young tree. The barkcloth made from this plant was not as soft and white as the *wauke* tapa, with which it was usually mixed. According to native informants it was used for the three traditional garments — the *malo* (loincloth), the *pa'u* (women's skirt) and the *kihei* (shoulder covering) — as well as for the *kapa moe* or sleeping tapa. The other wild-growing plants provided tapa of a lower quality which had a very restricted use.

Wauke trees were cut when they had reached a height of 1.8-3 metres (6-10 feet), with a lower diameter of about 2.5 cm (1 inch). The bark was then peeled off the trunk as a whole after which the green outer bark was removed from the inner bark by scraping or pulling it off. The inner bark was then soaked in sea-water for about ten days to make the material soft and easy to work and to give it the required white tint, for, according to one native informant, 'well made tapa must be clearer than moon-light, clearer than snow on the mountains'.

The bark of the other tapa-supplying plants was treated in a similar way. The *mamaki* bark, however, was soaked in fresh water, allegedly why its colour was not as white as the *wauke* material (which had been soaked in sea-water). The material was then given a preliminary beating with a club-shaped mallet which either had a smooth, rounded beating end, or was provided with

11. Hawaiian tapa beater *(i'e kuku)*. The grooved surface was used for beating, the patterned surface for watermarking the tapa. (Photograph: Rijksmuseum voor Volkenkunde, Leiden.)

three or four longitudinal panels, one of them smooth, the others having parallel ridges the width of which varied from panel to panel. When the beating was carried out with the latter type of mallet, the surface with the coarser ridges was used first, then those with finer ridges, and lastly the smooth surface.

After having been dried in the sun, to add still more to the brilliance of the white colour, these provisionally beaten bark strips were combined into groups of about five. Five of these groups of strips were taken together and soaked in fresh water for part of a day. Then followed fermentation, for which our native sources have mentioned two procedures, one in which the strips were wrapped in leaves and kept in a closed bowl for ten days or more, and the other consisting of keeping them between banana leaves in a shady place. These mounds of tapa bundles covered with leaves and stones resembled the mounds of the *imu* or earth ovens.

The beating took place in specially built houses, the size of which depended on the number of workers. The principal tools were again the tapa beater and the anvil or *kua*. There were two kinds of *kua*: the stone anvil which was used in the first stage of the beating with the rounded club-like mallet, and the wooden anvil used for further processing. The latter consisted of a log, about 1.7 metres (6 feet) long, with a nearly quadrangular cross-section and with the upper surface projecting beyond the lower surface at both ends like the prow and stern of a boat. The under-side was made hollow by a longitudinal groove, which made the anvil highly resonant. The tone varied between anvils and each woman's *kua* had its own sound. It is said that tapa-making women were able to convey messages over great distances by producing a special rhythmic beating as a well understood code of signals.

Just as in Tahiti, the beaters (*i'e kuku*) were four-sided wooden

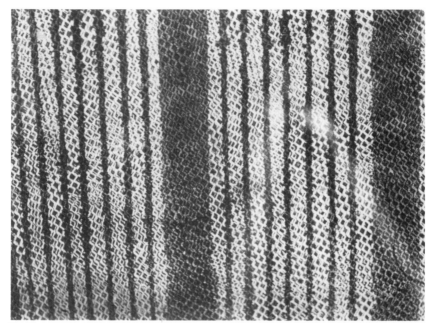

12. Fragment of Hawaiian tapa with watermark pattern. (Peabody Museum, Salem, Massachusetts.)

mallets with rounded handles and surfaces with a varying number of grooves. Here also, the beating started with coarsely grooved surfaces and, as the process advanced, surfaces with increasingly finer grooves and ridges were used. In the last stage of the beating process smooth surfaces served to make the cloth flat and even. The manufacture, as well as the decoration, of tapa reached its highest technical level during the nineteenth century. This development was probably mainly due to the use of new refined types of beaters made by Hawaiian woodcarvers after the introduction of metal tools. The surfaces of many of these *i'e* show a wide variety of designs, most of them of a geometrical nature, formed by combinations of incised lines (figure 11). These designs were impressed on the cloth and the pattern on the beater's surface appeared as a watermark in the tapa (figure 12). Since the overall pattern of these watermarked tapa is formed by a continuous, regular network of designs, the beater had to be laid on the cloth and then pressed down or hammered, each imprint fitting closely to the next.

The Hawaiian watermarking technique was unique in

Polynesia. In Indonesia, particularly in the cultures of eastern Indonesia in which tapa was an important element, Hawaiian watermarking had its counterpart in the Toraja of central Celebes (Sulawesi). There, just as in Hawaii, the manufacture and decoration of barkcloth had reached a high level of technical development.

The finished barkcloth was spread in the sun to dry, the edges weighted down with stones. In a Hawaiian legend the clouds are identified with drying sheets of tapa laid out in the sky by the goddess Hina who was a great tapa maker. When heavy winds blew the cloud tapas upward, the stones rolled off and the sound they made was called thunder by mortals. Another legend, also connected with Hina, says that she could not get her tapa dry because the days were too short. To help her, her son Maui snared the sun and broke off its long rays, robbing it of its extreme strength and speed so that the days lasted longer.

The beating was sometimes combined with felting together pieces of barkcloth, for example when sheets more than 20 metres (65 feet) long were required for ceremonial purposes. Pieces of tapa were also sewn together using a needle of bone, wood or bamboo and a thread made of tapa fibre. The *malo*, for instance, which was wound around the loins and hung down at the front and the back, was usually completed by stitching together the top ends of two beaten strips, each with a length of about 1.6 metres (5 feet), the height of a medium-sized paper mulberry tree. The sheets of the *kapa moe* or sleeping tapa (see below) were also joined by sewing.

Many of the *malo* and the *pa'u*, the women's skirts, were made of tapa with a regularly ribbed appearance resembling the coarsely grooved surface of a beater. A board or an anvil with such a surface was used to apply the ribbing. The dampened tapa was placed over it and a bamboo ruler was pressed against the tapa parallel to the grooves and ridges of the underlying wood. Another tool, the grooving instrument, which had a narrow edge like a skate, was then pressed back and forth along the ruler, forcing the cloth into the underlying groove. Repetition of this operation, after moving the ruler to the next groove, gave the cloth its ribbed appearance. This work was done not by women, but by men.

Decoration of tapa

The Hawaiian tapa makers had a wide choice of colours for the decoration of their cloths: the fertile islands offered them an

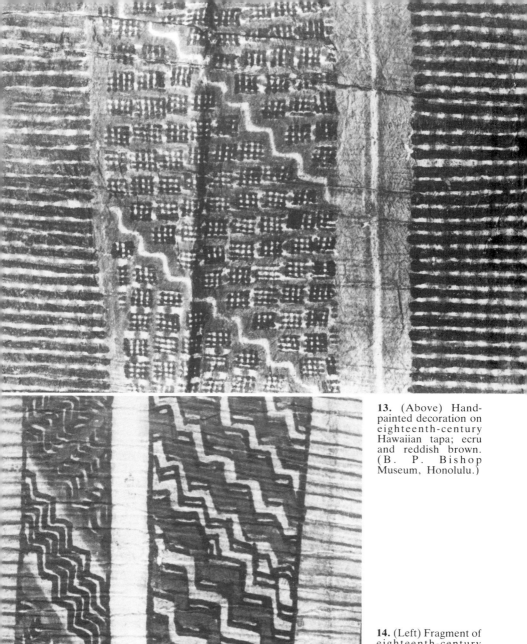

13. (Above) Hand-painted decoration on eighteenth-century Hawaiian tapa; ecru and reddish brown. (B. P. Bishop Museum, Honolulu.)

14. (Left) Fragment of eighteenth-century Hawaiian tapa, hand-painted; ecru, brown and black. (B. P. Bishop Museum, Honolulu.)

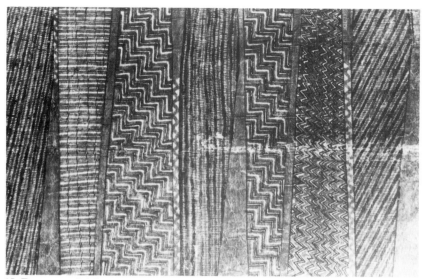

15. Fragment of eighteenth-century Hawaiian tapa, hand-painted; ecru, brown and black. (Canterbury Museum, Christchurch, New Zealand.)

abundant supply of plants to use for this purpose. The main source of brown dye was the bark of the *kuku* or candlenut tree. Black dye was also obtained primarily from this tree, from the nuts and the roots. Five trees and two kinds of ferns are mentioned as providing a red dye. Among the trees was the *noni* (*Morinda citrifolia*) which was used for colouring a special kind of tapa called *maluna*. *Maluna* tapas were often reserved for chiefs, in which case they were made under conditions of strict taboo. A yellow colouring matter was provided by three plants, one of them being the turmeric (*'olena*). In addition to these basic colours, pink, green, blue and grey dyes were used, also obtained from vegetable sources. Colouring materials originating from minerals were the red and yellow ochres. They were pounded to a powder and mixed with oil.

The Hawaiians customarily scented their tapas. This could be done either by adding the perfume to the colouring matter before its application or by perfuming the finished cloth in its entirety. A yellow dye for decorating the *malo* of chiefs was scented by mixing it with the liquid obtained from a sweet-smelling fern, the dye having become 'as subtly fragrant as the cool fragrance of the mountains'. Ingredients from a considerable number of plants, including the Hawaiian species of sandalwood, were used for scenting the finished barkcloth. These materials were strewn between the sheets of tapa or placed in the closed gourds in which tapas were stored.

The oldest known Hawaiian tapas were collected during Cook's third voyage. That they were decorated with freehand work is obvious from the nature of their bold and simple patterns and is moreover explicitly stated in a 1779 entry in a journal. The cloth, matching the style of decoration, is thick and rather stiff since it has not been subjected to hammering with patterned beater surfaces and watermarking, which gave the nineteenth-century tapas their characteristic refinement. For drawing, 'pieces of bamboo cane' were used which were dipped into paint and employed as pens (figures 13-16).

In nineteenth-century collections, these bamboo liners or pens occur in a far more refined form. Two types can be distinguished: single and multi-line pens, which usually resemble a fork with two or more prongs. Rulers were used to produce firm, straight lines. Many nineteenth-century tapas have decorated patterns applied by printing (figure 17). This was done by means of a printing block, a length of bamboo provided with a geometrical design at the top. This was carved on the inner unglazed surface, which could be worked easily. These carvings show a very large number of patterns and variations. The same figure was applied in continuous repetition and the resulting pattern on the printed barkcloth consists of long strips or stripes, to form the unbroken lines of which the tapa maker had to place the stamp very carefully each time.

Although a printing technique for tapa decoration was used in Tahiti (by means of leaves dipped into a dye and pressed on the cloth), block printing as practised in nineteenth-century Hawaii was unique in Polynesia. It was a phenomenon of tapa manufacture also found in Indonesia but was restricted, like the watermarking technique, to the Toraja of central Celebes (Sulawesi).

Tapas decorated by block printing were produced in large quantities. Production had probably been intensified by the consolidation of the Hawaiian state between 1794 and 1810 and the establishment of the royal court in Honolulu, which King Kamehameha I chose as his residence. At this court, where dancing was one of the integral parts of life, there was found a concentration of the *hula* troupes previously patronised by the local chiefs. This local intensification of the *hula* ceremonies led to an increasing demand for the sarong-like *hula* skirt, the

16. (Right) Fragment of eighteenth-century Hawaiian tapa, hand-painted; ecru, reddish brown and black. (Rijksmuseum voor Volkenkunde, Leiden.)

17. (Below) Printed pattern on a nineteenth-century Hawaiian tapa; ecru, red and black. (B. P. Bishop Museum, Honolulu.)

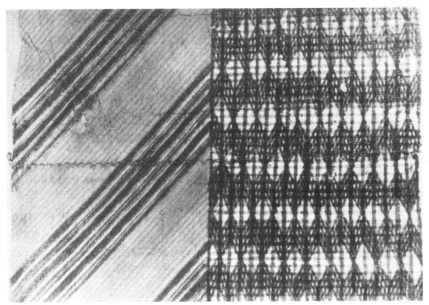

18. Part of a Hawaiian loincloth (*kapa malo*). The photograph shows the width of the garment, which is 28 cm (11 inches). Its length is 233 cm (7 feet 7 inches). It consists of two strips, each about half that length, which are joined by the seam visible in the middle. Rulers were used for the straight lines and printing blocks for the rows of chevron-like designs. Ecru, brown, reddish brown and black. (Peabody Museum, Salem, Massachusetts.)

essential garment of the female dancers. The need to meet this demand probably explains why the tapa makers changed over to block printing as the easiest and quickest method of decoration. The technique was then also applied to ordinary garments. This development probably induced the specialised craftsmen who made the printing blocks to increase their production of these tools and to extend the diversity of the stamp designs.

Another unique technique for colouring and decorating tapa consisted of placing a coloured layer on an uncoloured surface and then hammering the former into the latter to produce a tapa with a coloured and an uncoloured surface. These overlaid tapas were strong and could even be rinsed with water. The upper layer of some of the multi-layered *kapa moe* or sleeping tapas was made in this way and was thus stronger and thicker than the underlying, uncoloured sheets. Some overlaid tapas have an upper surface consisting of a field of coloured spots resulting from hammering in a very thin coloured sheet or coloured fragments. When a thin dark brown or black tapa with a perforated design was pounded on to a plain tapa, the finished product showed a pattern of light elements set off by a dark background.

Uses of tapa

In ancient Hawaii, barkcloth was used for a wide variety of purposes, embracing ordinary daily life, as well as ceremonial and religious aspects of the culture. It must have been made in large quantities.

The main object of tapa production was the making of clothing. As mentioned above, the three main types of garments were the *malo* or loincloth, the women's skirt (*pa'u*) and the *kihei* or shoulder covering. The *malo* (figure 18) consisted of a long strip of tapa usually made by stitching together two separate strips. It was wound around the loins and hung down at the front and the back. There were various kinds of *malo,* each of which had its own name. These names were sometimes related to the patterns and motifs imprinted on the *malo* and also to the colours used for the ornamentation. A very special kind was the yellow *malo.* Coloured with a dye from the turmeric and scented, it served as one of the chiefly status symbols.

The wearing of *malo* was not restricted to mortals. During the ritual of the initiation of a sacred place, a *heiau,* a brilliantly white *malo* which had been bleached in sea-water, was presented to the god Ku, to whom the *heiau* was consecrated. This *malo,* an attribute of the deified ruler and called '*malo* of the king', was carried to the sacred place by the female chiefs and finally wrapped around the carved figure of the god. The wrapping of a god figure was a regular religious practice. It was a sign or symbol of the god having entered the image, for the image itself had no special value: it became sacred only when it was occupied by the god. He could therefore only be approached after his carved figure had been dressed in fine white tapa. Before speaking to the priests the gods were also believed to enter into tall obelisk-shaped towers erected in the *heiau;* these towers were also covered with a fine white tapa. Since the *heiau* were often situated on the coast they also served as landmarks for canoe voyagers.

The *pa'u* worn by the women was a wrap-around sarong. It had a rectangular shape and was about 4 metres (13 feet) long and about a metre (3 feet) wide, reaching from waist to knee. Just as for the *malo,* the names applied to the *pa'u* were as diverse as

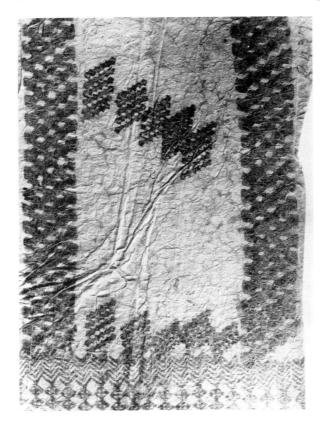

19. Part of the upper layer (*kilohana*) of a sleeping tapa (*kapa moe*); printed pattern, ecru and black. (B. P. Bishop Museum, Honolulu.)

their decorative patterns, some of them deriving from the dyes used for the ornamentation. In addition to the *pa'u* worn as ordinary daily clothing, there were two ceremonial varieties, the richly decorated *pa'u hula* and sarong-like garments of extraordinary length. The *pa'u hula,* the festive skirt worn by the *hula* dancers, bears elaborate block-printed ornamentation. The other variant was a ceremonial garment worn by high-ranking women, which sometimes achieved enormous proportions. On the occasion of the commemoration of the death of King Kamehameha I, Kamamalu, the wife of King Liholiho, wore a *pa'u* which had a normal width but was so long that, to don it, the cloth had to be spread out on the ground, 'where, beginning at one end, she laid her body across it, and rolled herself over and over till she had rolled the whole around her'. The garment was wound in this way around the waist about seventy times. A similar ceremonial *pa'u* collected by the same eye-witness is about 300 metres (1000 feet) long. It was believed that Pele, the volcano goddess of the island of Hawaii, presented her sister Hiiaka with such a *pa'u* and that it had the power of lightning when the goddess whirled it.

The *kihei* was a tapa cape which was worn over the left shoulder and fastened by tying the two top corners in a knot on the right shoulder.

A considerable proportion of the tapa production went to the large sleeping tapas or *kapa moe*. These consisted of a number of layers, ranging approximately from five to ten, which were attached to each other by stitching on one of the long sides, so that they could be turned like the pages of a book and the sleeper could cover himself with as many layers as the temperature of the night air required. The proportions were adjusted to the size and the number of sleepers and thus show a great deal of variation. The upper layer (*kilohana*) is usually the only one decorated (figure 19). Some *kilohana* are overlaid tapas, coloured on one side and stronger and thicker than the other sheets. Others show ornamentation formed by drawn lines and printed designs.

In addition to being worn as clothing by both mortal people and gods, tapa was put to a wide variety of practical uses. Tapa sheets served as house partitions and as a protection against mosquitoes. Decorated tapa covered the inner side of the house's thatch and the walls of the open porch. Thick-ribbed tapa was used as a floor covering. The wicks for stone lamps were made of tapa and it was used as a slow match that would stay lit for a long time in a period in which fire was made with fire sticks. Tapa had a medical use as bandages and was also used to make kites. In the early days of the missions tapa served for the binding of books.

The influx of foreigners and the processes of Westernisation and Christianisation eventually led to the extinction of this native handicraft. In the mid 1860s only the plainer forms of tapa were still worn in outlying districts and in 1890, when the B. P. Bishop Museum in Honolulu was opened, both manufacture and use of tapa had almost ceased. Now the sound of the beater is no longer heard and the art of making and decorating barkcloth, once a highlight of Hawaiian material culture, has completely disappeared.

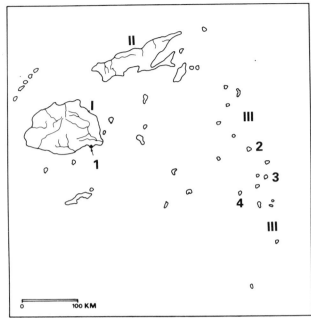

20. Sketch map of Fiji. I Viti Levu; II Vanua Levu; III Lau Group. 1 Suva; 2 Lakemba; 3 Mothe; 4 Kambara.

21. (Below) Mothe Island in the Lau Group, Fiji. Mothe is a 'high' island. Its shape is more or less elliptical with a length of about 4 km (2½ miles). The inhabitants, about 500 people in 1973, are concentrated in a complex of three villages on the southeast coast.

5
Mothe Island, Fiji

In the barkcloth production of Mothe Island (figures 20 and 21) two types of tapa can be distinguished, cloths named *masi,* the general Fijian term for barkcloth, and tapas called *ngatu vakatonga, ngatu* being the Tongan name for tapa and *vakatonga* meaning 'in the Tongan way'.

The Fijian *masi* or *masi kesa, kesa* being the name of the principal dye, are decorated by stencilling, a technique of tapa ornamentation which is unique in Oceania (figures 22 and 23). The decoration of these tapas consists of a limited number of stencilled designs applied in continuous repetition and generally forming a straight-lined pattern covering the entire surface (figure 24). Occasionally the decorative pattern of *masi kesa* consists of a composition of isolated, rosette-like figures (figures 25 and 26). The technique involved and the nature of their decoration make the *masi* a separate type of Oceanic tapa, standing apart from the barkcloth made in the neighbouring islands of western Polynesia. For that reason, it is not discussed here (but see the author's *Tapa on Moce Island, Fiji*).

The *ngatu vakatonga* (figure 27) are long, runner-like sheets which are, both technically and functionally, very similar to the primary type of barkcloth produced in Tonga. Their manufacture and decoration, as well as the uses to which they are put, is therefore compared with those of their Polynesian counterparts in Tahiti and Hawaii.

Manufacture of ngatu

The only plant on Mothe supplying the raw material for the production of barkcloth is the paper mulberry or *masi,* from which the typically Fijian kind of tapa derives its name. In earlier times, when tapa was made to meet the needs of the islanders only, the trees were planted in vegetable gardens. In the 1960s increasing amounts of small stencil-decorated *masi* were produced for the tourist market and separate *masi* gardens started to be established. By 1973 cultivation was concentrated in a grove complex containing more than a hundred plots.

Fully grown *masi* trees are 2-3 metres (6-10 feet) high and have a diameter of 2-3 cm (about 1 inch). Mature trees with straight stems provide bark of the highest quality for the manufacture of stencilled tapa for use on ceremonial occasions. Bark of lower

22. (Above) Mothe Island tapa (*masi kesa*) with stencilled decoration; black, white and brown.

23. (Left) Stencilled Mothe Island tapa for ceremonial use called *ngatu vakaviti*; black, white and reddish brown. In the house where a traditional wedding is celebrated it forms the partition of the chamber arranged for the bridal couple and also serves as the background against which the bride and groom sit in state. This tapa carries the name of the groom, who was married on 23rd May 1973. The young woman is one of his relatives and played a leading part in the making and decoration of the tapa; the other woman is her mother.

24. Stencilling the *masi kesa.*

quality, often supplied by immature and crooked trees, is used for the production of the commercial tapas. It is also used for the making of the *ngatu vakatonga,* since these cloths are not valued for their aesthetic qualities but for their dimensions.

The procedure of preparing the bark follows the general Polynesian pattern. The work starts with the cutting of the tree, the peeling of the trunk and the separation of the inner and the outer bark. Mallets (*ike*) and anvils (*ndundua*) are the main tools used by the women for the beating. The *ike* are four-sided with rounded handles. Three beating surfaces are provided with longitudinal grooves; the fourth side is smooth. Two types of beater are in use, the *ike vakatonga* (figure 28), which is similar to its Tongan counterpart, and the 'Fijian' beater or *ike vakaviti* (figure 29). Though the latter is more slender and lighter than the 'Tongan' version, both types of *ike* are far less refined than those

25. (Above and below) Stencils (*draudrau*) of the rosette type cut by one of the two women who were the expert *draudrau* makers on Mothe Island. *Draudrau* means leaves: from ancient times this was the material from which they had been made. In 1973 X-ray films were used; these came from the capital, Suva, via family connections.

26. Tapa jacket with rosette-like stencilled figures. It was made and decorated by the best tapa makers of the island since it was meant to be part of the festive attire of a woman portraying the 'Queen of Mothe' at the Lau Islands Festival in Suva in August 1973.
27. A completed *ngatu vakatonga* spread out to dry in the sun.

28. (Above) A 'Tongan' beater (*ike vakatonga*). (Photograph: Rijksmuseum voor Volkenkunde, Leiden.)
29. (Below). A 'Fijian' beater (*ike vakaviti*). (Photograph: Rijksmuseum voor Volkenkunde, Leiden.)

formerly used in Tahiti and Hawaii. The grooving is much coarser, the number of grooves is approximately three for the 'Tongan' compared with six for the 'Fijian' *ike,* and the number of grooves does not differ between surfaces. The *ndundua* are two-footed and are on average 2 metres (6 feet) long and 30 cm (1 foot) wide. *Ike* and *ndundua* are made of hard wood from tree species which are very scarce, or do not occur, on Mothe. Like most of the wooden implements in use on the island, as well as the boats, they were made on islands in the southern part of the Lau Group where there are trees which supply the necessary kind of strong, hard wood and woodworking has become a local specialisation.

The procedure for the manufacture of the 'Tongan' tapa consists of two stages, the making of the standard strips needed for assembling and the combined process of assembling and decoration. For the manufacture of the standard strips the inner bark is laid across the width of the anvil and beaten over the entire length until the original strip is about five times wider

30. Beating the bark strips, initial stage. The two women practice *veilali*, rhythmical beating in which the sound is as important as the hammering of the bark strips. The beating is usually done individually.

31. After about half an hour of almost continuous beating the width of the strips has increased considerably.

(figures 30 and 31). Two or three of these beaten strips are placed one above the other. Then follows a treatment consisting of folding and continued beating, which causes the pieces to fuse and increases their width. The final product is a strip about 170 cm (5 feet 6 inches) long and 60 cm (2 feet) wide, approximately ten times wider than the original bark strip. When preparing the Fijian *masi*, the women give the material its finishing touch by combining two of these sheets, which produces an even, supple cloth. For the manufacture of the *ngatu* this part of the process is omitted and the quality of the strips is therefore distinctly lower than that of the material for tapa of the Fijian type. The pieces thus made, which are the standard strips for the manufacture of the *ngatu vakatonga*, are darker than the *masi kesa* and also comparatively stiff. The thickness is not uniform and the layers can often be distinguished because the superficial beating has led to inadequate felting. The ecru colour is not a problem because the entire surface is to be treated with a brownish fluid. Neither are the other seemingly negative characteristics of these strips found objectionable since the standards for the evaluation of the final product differ widely from those applied to the *masi kesa*.

32. Design tablets (*kupeti*). The one above is said to have been made on Mothe about 1880. The one below was made by an elderly woman still alive in 1973. The figure is called *vakamata*, 'provided with eyes' (*mata*, eye).

Assembling and ornamentation of ngatu

When the number of standard strips needed for the *ngatu* has been completed, the women are ready to start the next phase of the process. Unlike the production of the *masi kesa*, which is carried out by each tapa worker individually, the task of decorating the strips and simultaneously joining them together into a long 'runner' is a combined effort of about seven to ten women. During the work they sit cross-legged along both sides of a long wooden plank (*papa*) about 4 metres (13 feet) long placed in the middle of the working space, a house or a lean-to providing shade and protection against the rain.

The *papa* consists of the upturned middle part of a dugout canoe, which provides a convex upper surface approximately 40 cm (16 inches) wide and raised from the ground on stones and empty kerosene cans. A wide-meshed European fishing net is stretched over the *papa,* covering its entire width. It is about 60 cm (2 feet) shorter than the tapa to be placed on the *papa* because a 30 cm (1 foot) wide border on each side of the barkcloth is not decorated. Design tablets or *kupeti* (figure 32), mainly consisting of pieces of leaf or leaf-sheath with an 'embroidered' design in relief, are fastened to the net. The great majority of these *kupeti* are rectangular, measuring from 25 to 70 cm (10 to 27 inches) in length and from 15 to 40 cm (6 to 16 inches) in width. They have a base of strips of *Pandanus* leaf sewn together. A relief pattern formed by flexible fresh coconut-leaflet mid-ribs, which resemble thick needles, is sewn down on the rectangular base in the desired pattern. These patterns are linear and rectangular in their main outlines; within these, curvilinear and other less severe motifs are applied. In some cases, the leaf *kupeti* have the shape of the decorative motif itself, for example, a flower, a butterfly, a fan or a crown.

When the net has been stretched over the *papa* and the *kupeti* have been placed on the net and fastened to it, one of the standard strips is laid lengthwise over the *papa,* covering the net and the *kupeti*. Next, the women sitting on both sides of the *papa* rub over the surface of the barkcloth with a wad soaked in a brown dye made from the bark of the *dongo* tree (*Rizophora mangle*), a mangrove species. The figuration of the net and the relief designs of the *kupeti* are thus rubbed into the cloth and appear on the upper surface as a pattern consisting of dark brown lines and stripes, reproducing the meshes of the net and the designs of the *kupeti* against a lighter toned ground which is only superficially coloured.

33. Working around the *papa*. The design patterns of the net and the *kupeti* have been rubbed into the standard strip. Another strip is being spread over the *papa*, partly overlapping the first one, to which it will be glued.

34. The new strip is glued to the one already given its pattern. The cloth will now be pushed over the *papa* to the right and the same underlying pattern will be rubbed into the new strip.

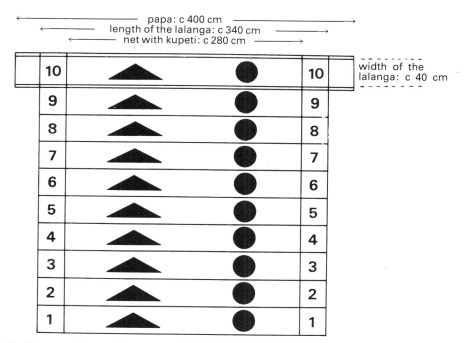

35. The assembling of the *ngatu vakatonga* on the *papa*.

When this work is finished, the strip is pushed across the width of the *papa* and a new strip of the same size is glued to it with a paste prepared from boiled manioc tubers (figures 33 and 34). This strip is given the same treatment. The procedure of pasting and rubbing is repeated many times so that a long runner-like tapa is produced. Since the standard strips are placed lengthwise on the *papa* and the strips are joined by pasting together the overlapping parts at the longitudinal sides, the width of the *ngatu* corresponds to the length of the strips. The length of the cloth is determined by the number of strips pasted together and given the *kupeti* pattern.

As mentioned above, the length of the net covering the *papa* is about 60 cm (2 feet) less than the length of the standard strips. These are placed on the net in such a way that at each end an area of about 30 cm (1 foot) long extends beyond the net. Because the rubbing of the strip is restricted to the part which covers the net, the two outer parts of the strip are left uncoloured. On the completed *ngatu*, these areas show as uncoloured, undecorated

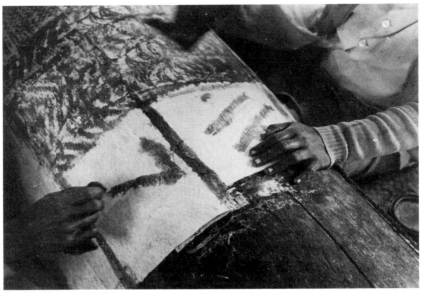

36. Numbering the *lalanga.*

borders on both sides (figure 35).

The decorated part of the *ngatu* consists of a repetition of the same design unit, formed by net and *kupeti,* which is called *lalanga.* The *lalanga* appear crosswise, positioned as the rungs of a ladder, on the completed tapa. The length of a *ngatu* is measured by the number of its *lalanga,* which is made manifest by the application of the number of each *lalanga* on the adjacent sections of uncoloured border (figure 36). This method of indicating the length of the *ngatu* is a result of Western influence and is a relatively recent development in barkcloth manufacture on Mothe. Nevertheless these numbers are an important element in the decoration. As mentioned before, *ngatu* are not valued by their aesthetic qualities: it is their length which is crucial and which is given full attention when the tapa is shown in public on ceremonial occasions. It is then carried and presented in such a manner that the last *lalanga* with the highest number is in front. These festive tapas often have a length of 50-60 *lalanga* or 20-30 metres (60-90 feet).

When the work on and around the *papa* has been finished, the tapa is spread out on the grass to dry. It is then given its final treatment by the same group of women. Kneeling on the cloth

37. Painting over the main lines of the rubbed pattern of the 58th *lalanga*.

38. The *ngatu* shown on figure 37 after its completion. The last number on the border shows that it is 61 *lalanga* long.

and with the help of a pointed stick and a container of *dongo* dye, they paint over the main lines of the shadowy rubbed pattern with its vague figuration (figures 37 and 38).

Uses of ngatu

Ngatu vakatonga play an important part in the *vakataraisulu* ceremony, which marks the end of a hundred-day mourning period (figure 39). The *ngatu* for such a feast which took place on the island in 1973 was made by relatives of the deceased, who had been a high-ranking chief. At the climax of the feast, in which the whole population participated, the tapa was presented to the chief of the island. Relatives of the deceased, male and female, took a prominent place in the presentation. This was performed by two rows of people who lined up on each side of the *ngatu*, picked up the cloth and walked slowly past the admiring throng toward the chief and his men. The *ngatu*, waving and ballooning in the wind, expressly demonstrated its length by the *lalanga* numbers in front (60, 59, 58 . . .) so that all present, and the important guests in particular, were immediately confronted by its impressive dimensions. The official presentation of the *ngatu* to the chief was made by the *vakavanua*, the headman of the

39. The *ngatu vakatonga* shown on figures 37 and 38 is ceremonially presented at a *vakataraisulu.*

deceased man's village. His formal speech was answered by the *matanivanua*, the chief's 'herald', who acts and speaks on behalf of the latter on official occasions. The chief then ordered the tapa to be cut up and distributed among the rightful claimants. Those who received a part of the *ngatu* folded it up, wrapped it in matting and carefully preserved it as a highly valued piece of property.

Just as the stencilled 'Fijian' tapa or *masi kesa* is produced for the tourist market in great quantities, the *ngatu,* in addition to their ceremonial role, also have an economic function. Unlike the *masi kesa,* they are not a source of cash income because foreign visitors to Fiji are not interested in pieces of these brownish, rather carelessly made tapas with their vague *lalanga* designs. However, in the traditional barter system, the trade between the people of Mothe and the inhabitants of other islands, they play an important part. Various kinds of mats, for instance, are exchanged for pieces of *ngatu.* These mats, plaited of *Pandanus* leaf strips and sometimes decorated along the edges by a fringed border made of woollen yarn of various colours, are provided by the women of the Lau Islands of Lakemba and Kambara where mat plaiting is a specialisation. In the bargains thus made large groups of relatives are involved on both sides. In 1973 money had not entered into the traditional barter system within the Lau Group. In bargaining with the Fijians living in the capital, Suva, however, mention was made of a cash value for a *ngatu* or pieces of one: a price of 1 Fijian dollar per *lalanga* was charged.

Occasionally a group of enterprising women forms a *kambani*, a temporary work-group in which they cooperate in making a stock of *ngatu*. This is reserved as capital until there is an occasion to use it for the acquisition of certain goods.

6
Tapa: common patterns and differences

Common patterns

The descriptions given above of the manufacture, decoration and uses of barkcloth in three different island societies make it evident that Polynesian tapa displays a number of common basic traits: the use of the inner bark of the specially cultivated paper mulberry tree as the main source of the material, the beating of the bark on a wooden anvil and with four-sided wooden mallets provided with grooved beating surfaces, the joining of the beaten strips to form sizable sheets, the decoration of these sheets by the application of dyes extracted from trees and shrubs and the use of these decorated tapas as clothing and for ceremonial purposes.

Differences

Within this common pattern, however, many differences appear to have existed between the tapa of Tahiti and Hawaii, representing central and northern Polynesia, on the one hand, and Mothe Island, as the western Polynesian example, on the other. In Tahiti and Hawaii, the bark strips were fermented before being beaten for several days. This made the beating more effective and added to the quality of the tapa. The hammering was done very thoroughly with the use of refined beaters with approximately five to seven times more grooves than the Mothe Island *ike*. In eighteenth-century Hawaii *i'e* with patterned surfaces were used for watermarking the tapa in the final stage of beating. To make larger sheets, the beaten strips were usually joined by felting together the overlapping edges, thus forming a beautiful, coherent cloth.

On Mothe Island, the bark strips are not subjected to fermentation. The material for the *ngatu vakatonga,* the typical western Polynesian version of the Fijian tapa, is beaten out carelessly with the coarsely grooved *ike* and the quality of the cloth made is far inferior to the Tahitian *ahu* and the Hawaiian *kapa.* The beaten strips are not felted together but are joined by pasting, which gives a less coherent cloth. Its component parts can often be distinguished, particularly when the pasting is done in a careless manner, which is the usual practice.

The methods of decoration and the nature of the designs and patterns used also differ greatly between the two areas. In ancient Tahiti and eighteenth-century Hawaii, the decoration was applied to the tapa with meticulous care and artistic refinement. The leaf-printed tapa clothing of the early contact period in Tahiti and the block-printed, watermarked Hawaiian barkcloth, though technically dissimilar, both represent the highest development in Polynesian tapa decoration.

The decorative pattern of the long, runner-like tapas of western Polynesia, formed in ladder-like repetition by the *kupeti* designs, is of little interest from an aesthetic point of view. However, this kind of decoration is not meant to arouse the admiration of onlookers: it is the repetition of the same design unit and the application of its number on the uncoloured borders which are the essential characteristics of the *ngatu*.

The most important aspect of this tapa is its spectacular size and the impression made by the piece as a whole. When it is carried and offered to the principal guests at a public ceremony, it is the length of the *ngatu* which really matters. The feasts of which these tapas constitute an essential part occur frequently in western Polynesia and the Lau Islands of Fiji. It is highly probable, therefore, that the special semi-mechanical techniques for the manufacture and decoration of barkcloth practised in these areas specifically were developed to cope with the demand for ornamented tapa sheets of a spectacular size for use on ceremonial occasions.

In Tahiti and Hawaii, there also existed this interrelationship between the techniques of manufacture and decoration, the size of the tapas and their design patterns, on the one hand, and their function in society, on the other. The refined techniques of ornamentation, as well as the aesthetic qualities of the designs and patterns, meticulously applied to the cloth, were closely linked to the uses to which tapa was put. Decorated tapas were worn as festive clothing and, when donned by high-ranking people, they served to indicate social status. Public attention was focused on the wearers of these tapas, which were thus looked at and evaluated by every member of the village community. They were therefore made and decorated with great care. This held to a still greater degree for the tapas in which the god figures were wrapped during religious ceremonies.

This social integration of tapa probably contributed a great deal to the survival of barkcloth manufacture in western Polynesia and its complete extinction in the central and northern areas, particularly Tahiti and Hawaii. On the latter islands, tapa was used mainly as clothing and for magical and religious purposes. We have seen that in Hawaii new techniques of decoration (watermarking, block printing) were developed after the introduction of metal tools in the early contact period. The enrichment of tapa decoration by the leaf-printing technique in the similar stage of Tahitian history may perhaps also be attributed to Western influence. One of the material aspects of the Westernisation process, however, was the introduction of textile clothing, which was accepted with enthusiasm. The tapa garments were soon replaced by cotton prints and thus one of the two most important pillars that had supported the structure of tapa production was undermined. The second pillar, the function of tapa in religious feasts and ceremonies, was fiercely attacked by the missionaries. With the success of the missions and the resulting conversions to Christianity, the traditional gods were no longer worshipped and their images disappeared, together with the festive associations in which tapa played such an important part. The other use to which tapa was put, that is, to demonstrate the status of people of rank, did not prove to be sufficiently vital to prevent the disintegration of tapa manufacture. In Tahiti no tapa has been produced since about 1830 and in Hawaii even the oldest inhabitants no longer know how to make it. The splendid

40. The author and his wife in one of the paper mulberry gardens on Mothe Island, Fiji. (Photograph: Steven Symonds.)

tapas of these islands can now only be admired in museums.

From the Mothe example, which is typical of tapa in western Polynesia, it is evident that the semi-mechanical production of *ngatu* is still being practised and that these tapas still have an essential function of great importance in society. They are the principal gifts in ceremonial presentations in which the whole village community participates. These presentations are the highlight of a system of exchange of material goods and services which forms a link of vital significance between individuals and groups. This system, as a network of human relationships, was acceptable to the missionaries and did not meet with any serious resistance from Christianity. This is probably the main reason for the survival of tapa in western Polynesia to the present day as a well integrated element in social life.

7
Museums to visit

Most museums with ethnographical collections have some Polynesian and Fijian barkcloth. The museums listed below are the principal ones with whose tapa collections the author became familiar during his researches.

United Kingdom
Cambridge University Museum of Archaeology and Anthropology, Downing Street, Cambridge CB2 3DZ. Telephone: 0223 337733.

Horniman Museum, London Road, Forest Hill, London SE23 3PQ. Telephone: 01-699 1872 or 2339 or 4911.

Museum of Mankind (Ethnography Department of the British Museum), 6 Burlington Gardens, London W1X 2EX. Telephone: 01-437 2224 or 2228.

Pitt Rivers Museum, South Parks Road, Oxford OX1 3PP. Telephone: Oxford (0865) 270927.

Royal Museum of Scotland, Chambers Street, Edinburgh EH1 1JF. Telephone: 031-225 7534.

Australia
Australian Museum, 6-8 College Street, Sydney, New South Wales 2000.

National Museum of Victoria, 258-321 Russell Street, Melbourne, Victoria 3000.

Austria
Museum für Völkerkunde, Heldenplatz 3, Neue Hofburg, 1010 Vienna 1.

Fiji
Fiji Museum, Government Buildings, POB 2023, Suva.

France
Musée de l'Homme, Palais de Chaillot, Place du Trocadéro, 75016 Paris.

Musée des Arts Africains et Océaniens, 293 Avenue Daumesnil, 75012 Paris.

Germany
Hamburgisches Museum für Völkerkunde, Rothenbaumchaussee 64, 2000 Hamburg 13.
Museum für Völkerkunde, Arnimallee 23-27, 1000 Berlin 33.
Rautenstrauch-Joest Museum, Ubierring 45, 5000 Cologne.

Hawaii
Bernice Pauahi Bishop Museum, 1355 Kalihi Street, Honolulu HI 96819.

Netherlands
Koninklijk Instituut voor de Tropen (Tropenmuseum), Linnaeusstraat 2, 1092 AD Amsterdam.
Museum voor Volkenkunde, Willemskade 25, 3016 DM Rotterdam.
Rijksmuseum voor Volkenkunde, Steenstraat 1, 2300 AE Leiden.
Volkenkundig Museum Nusantara, St Agathaplein 4, 2611 HR Delft.

New Caledonia
Musée de Nouvelle Calédonie, Nouméa.

New Zealand
Auckland Institute and Museum (Auckland War Memorial Museum), The Domain, Auckland 1.
Canterbury Museum, Rolleston Avenue, Christchurch 1.
National Museum, Buckle Street, Wellington.
Otago Museum, Great King Street, Dunedin.

United States of America
American Museum of Natural History, 79th Street and Central Park West, New York, NY 10024.
Field Museum of Natural History, Roosevelt Road at Lake Shore Drive, Chicago, Illinois 60605.
National Museum of Natural History (Smithsonian Institution), 10th Street and Constitution Avenue, NW, Washington DC 20560.
Peabody Museum of Archaeology and Ethnology, 11 Divinity Avenue, Cambridge, Massachusetts 02138.
Peabody Museum of Salem, 161 Essex Street, Salem, Massachusetts 01970.

8
Further reading

Beaglehole, J. C. *The Exploration of the Pacific*. Adam and Charles Black, 1947.

Bellwood, Peter. *Man's Conquest of the Pacific. The Prehistory of Southeast Asia and Oceania*. Collins, 1978.

Brigham, W. T. *Ka Hana Kapa. The Story of the Manufacture of Kapa (Tapa), or Bark-Cloth, in Polynesia and Elsewhere, but Especially in the Hawaiian Islands*. B. P. Bishop Museum Memoirs 3, 1911.

Buck, Peter H. *Vikings of the Pacific* (first published as *Vikings of the Sunrise*). University of Chicago Press, 1959.

Crocombe, Ron. *The South Pacific. An Introduction*. Longman Paul, 1983.

Cumberland, Kenneth B. *Southwest Pacific. A Geography of Australia, New Zealand and their Pacific Island Neighbourhoods*. Methuen, 1956.

Finney, Ben R. 'New Perspectives in Polynesian Voyaging' in Highland, Genevieve A., *et al.* (editors), *Polynesian Cultural History*. B. P. Bishop Museum Special Bulletin 39, 1967.

Golson, Jack (editor). *Polynesian Navigation*. Polynesian Society, 1963.

Haddon, A. C., and Hornell, James. *Canoes of Oceania* (3 volumes). B. P. Bishop Museum Special Publications 27-9, 1936-8.

Hambruch, P. *Oceanische Rindenstoffe*. Gerhard Stalling, 1926.

Heyerdahl, Thor. *American Indians in the Pacific*. George Allen and Unwin, 1952.

Kaeppler, Adrienne L. *The Fabrics of Hawaii (Bark Cloth)*. F. Lewis, 1975.

Kooijman, Simon. *Ornamented Bark-Cloth in Indonesia*. E. J. Brill, 1963.

— *Tapa in Polynesia*. B. P. Bishop Museum Bulletin 234, 1972.

— 'Tapa Techniques and Tapa Patterns in Polynesia: A Regional Differentiation' in Forge, Anthony (editor), *Primitive Art and Society*. Oxford University Press, 1973.

— *Tapa on Moce Island, Fiji. A Traditional Handicraft in a Changing Society*. E. J. Brill, 1977.

Leonard, Anne, and Terrell, John. *Patterns of Paradise. The Styles and Significance of Bark Cloth around the World*. Field Museum of Natural History, 1980.

Levison, Michael; Ward, R. Gerard; and Webb, John W. *The Settlement of Polynesia. A Computer Simulation.* The University of Minnesota Press, 1973.

Lewis, David. *We, the Navigators. The Ancient Art of Landfinding in the Pacific.* Australian National University Press, 1972.

Oliver, Douglas L. *The Pacific Islands.* The Natural History Library Edition, 1961.

Sharp, Andrew. *Ancient Voyagers in the Pacific.* Penguin Books, 1957.

Suggs, Robert C. *The Island Civilizations of Polynesia.* Mentor, The New American Library, 1960.

Thompson, Laura. *Southern Lau, Fiji. An Ethnography.* B. P. Bishop Museum Bulletin 162, 1940.

Index

Page numbers in italic refer to illustrations